ALEX THE CYBER HERO

STANDING UP TO UNKIND MESSAGES

By Sarah Miles

Contents

Introduction 5

Chapter 1: Meet Me, Alex the Cyber Hero 9

Chapter 2: A mysterious Friend requests 14

Chapter 3: Unkind Messages emerge 19

Chapter 4: Alex Activates the cyber hero plan 23

Chapter 5: talking to a trusted adult 30

Chapter 6: a positive turnaround 35

Chapter 7: Alex's Cyber safety tips for friends 40

Chapter 8: The Cyber hero code 56

Conclusion: Alex's Next Adventure 70

Bonus section for parents: Cyber safety tips 73

Alex the Cyber Hero

PRESENTED TO:

....

DATE: ....

Alex the Cyber Hero

INTRODUCTION

This story introduces children to the importance of cyber safety through the adventures of Alex,

Alex the Cyber Hero

a young superhero navigating the digital jungle. Alex encounters challenges when faced with unkind messages from a stranger. Parents can read along and discuss safety tips and strategies to empower their

Alex the Cyber Hero

children in the online world!

CHAPTER 1: MEET ME, ALEX THE CYBER HERO

Alex is a regular kid by day, but online, he transforms into a cyber hero! He

Alex the Cyber Hero

loves playing games, chatting with friends, and sharing cool pictures of his art in his online community. Alex's Secret: He knows that, just like in the real world, he must be smart and safe online. Today, however, Alex is about to encounter his biggest online challenge yet!

Alex the Cyber Hero

CHAPTER 2: A MYSTERIOUS FRIEND REQUESTS

One day, Alex receives a message from someone named "Mighty-Max," who says,

Alex the Cyber Hero

"Hey, I saw your game score—so cool! Wanna be friends?"

Hero Instincts:

While excited, Alex feels a twinge of caution.

Remembering his parents' advice, he asks, "Do I know you?"

Alex the Cyber Hero

CHAPTER 3: UNKIND MESSAGES EMERGE

Mighty-Max's friendly tone quickly shifts as he replies, "You're no fun!" Soon, he sends unkind messages like, "You'll never be as good as me!" and "You must be bad at games." Feeling

Hurt: Alex feels his heart sink. Proud of his gaming skills, he's confused and wonders,

Alex the Cyber Hero

"Did I do something wrong?"

CHAPTER 4: ALEX ACTIVATES THE CYBER HERO PLAN

Alex recalls his <u>Cyber Hero Plan:</u>

Stop, Block, Tell!

Stop: Alex pauses,

takes a deep breath, and reminds himself that he hasn't done anything wrong.

Block: He knows he doesn't have to tolerate unkind words.

Alex the Cyber Hero

He swiftly presses the "Block" button, stopping Mighty-Max from messaging him again.

Alex the Cyber Hero

Alex the Cyber Hero

<u>Tell:</u> Feeling empowered, Alex heads to talk to his parents, who have always encouraged him to come to

them if anything

feels off online.

Chapter 5: Talking to a Trusted Adult

Alex's mom listens intently as he explains the situation.

She smiles and reassures him, "You did the right thing, Alex! You're a true cyber hero for following your plan."

Learning Together: They discuss how some online users might not be who they claim to be. His mom reminds him that unkind words reflect more on the speaker than on him.

Alex the Cyber Hero

CHAPTER 6: A POSITIVE TURNAROUND

The next day, Alex feels a sense of pride. Instead of letting Mighty-

Alex the Cyber Hero

Max's words diminish him, he recognizes that he's stronger for addressing the situation.

New Perspective: When Alex logs into his game, he finds cheerful messages from real friends saying,

Alex the Cyber Hero

"Great game yesterday!" and "Let's play together soon!"

He smiles, knowing these are the connections that matter.

Chapter 7: Alex's Cyber Safety Tips for Friends

Alex's Advice: At school, Alex shares his experience with friends, offering his Cyber Hero

Tips:

1. Stop, Block, tell: If someone says something unkind, stop, block

them, and inform a trusted adult.

2. Be Proud of Who You Are: Remember, unkind words cannot change your true self.

3. Only Befriend People You Know:

Friends should enhance your happiness and sense of safety!

4. Protect Your Personal Information: Never share your passwords, address, school

name, or other personal details online.

5. Think Before You Click: Avoid clicking on unknown links or

accepting requests from strangers to prevent scams or viruses.

6. Use Strong Passwords: Create

Alex the Cyber Hero

unique passwords with letters, numbers, and symbols to keep your accounts secure.

7. Be Kind Online: Treat others how you want to be treated—kindness spreads positivity and helps build a

safe space for everyone.

8. Log Out When Using Shared Devices: Always log out after using a

computer or tablet at school, a library, or anywhere public.

Alex the Cyber Hero

Know That It's Okay to Take a Break: If the internet feels overwhelming, it's perfectly fine to

Alex the Cyber Hero

step away and do something you enjoy offline.

9. Learn and Share: Teach others these tips and work together to make the internet a

safer, happier place!

CHAPTER 8: THE CYBER HERO CODE

<u>A New Pledge:</u>

Inspired by Alex's experience, he and his friends create their own Cyber

Hero Code, vowing to:

CODE 1: Respect each other's feelings online.

Alex the Cyber Hero

CODE 2: Only engage with people they know and trust.

Alex the Cyber Hero

CODE 3: Always report to an adult if they feel uncomfortable online.

Alex the Cyber Hero

CODE 4: Speak up if they experience or witness bullying, threats, or any behavior that doesn't feel right.

Alex the Cyber Hero

CODE 5: Protect Their Privacy: Never share personal details like their address, school name, or

photos that reveal their location.

CODE 6: Stand Up Against Cyberbullying: Support friends

Alex the Cyber Hero

who might be targeted by online bullying by offering help and informing an adult.

Alex the Cyber Hero

CODE 7: Think Before Posting or Sharing: Always consider how a message or post

could affect others before sending it.

CODE 8: Be a Digital Role Model: Lead by example, encouraging positive and safe online behavior among peers.

CODE 9: Stay Alert for Scams and Tricks:

Alex the Cyber Hero

Recognize phishing attempts, fake profiles, and other online dangers, and avoid them.

Alex the Cyber Hero

CODE 10: Keep Devices and Accounts Secure: Use strong passwords, enable two-factor

Alex the Cyber Hero

authentication, and keep security software updated.

CONCLUSION: ALEX'S NEXT ADVENTURE

Moving Forward:

Alex understands that challenges will always arise, but he feels equipped and strong. As a Cyber Hero, he is ready to keep his online world safe and enjoyable,

Alex the Cyber Hero

facing whatever comes next!

BONUS SECTION FOR PARENTS: CYBER SAFETY TIPS

1. Keep Open Communication: Encourage children to share their

online experiences with you.

2. Reinforce the Stop, Block, Tell Method: Teach kids to respond

effectively to uncomfortable messages.

3. Stay Engaged: Regularly ask about their online friends

and experiences, fostering a supportive environment.

4. Set Clear Rules and Boundaries:

Define age-appropriate guidelines for screen time, app usage, and online interactions.

5. Teach Critical Thinking: Help kids identify suspicious links, fake profiles, and misleading content by asking

them to think critically about what they see online.

6. Be a Role Model: Demonstrate safe

and respectful online behavior, as children often mirror their parents' habits.

7. Install Parental Controls: Use tools to monitor and limit access to inappropriate content while

maintaining trust by explaining why these controls are in place.

8. Know the Platforms:

Familiarize yourself with the apps, games, and websites your children use to better understand potential risks and benefits.

9. Emphasize Privacy: Teach kids the importance of not sharing

personal information or photos that could compromise their safety.

Alex the Cyber Hero

10. Keep Devices in Shared Spaces: For younger children, consider keeping devices in common areas to easily

supervise their activities.

11. Discuss the Importance of Empathy Online: Teach children to

consider how their words and actions online can impact others emotionally.

12. Monitor for Signs of Trouble:

Alex the Cyber Hero

Be alert to changes in mood or behavior that may indicate your child is experiencing

cyberbullying or other online issues. By staying involved and proactive, parents can help their children

Alex the Cyber Hero

confidently explore the digital world while prioritizing safety and respect.

Alex the Cyber Hero

NOTE:

Foster a Safe Online Community: Work together to create an online space where

Alex the Cyber Hero

everyone feels welcome, valued, and safe.

www.ingramcontent.com/pod-product-compliance
Lightning Source LLC
Chambersburg PA
CBHW082253220526
45469CB00009B/2981